W9-CAE-983

21st Century Skills **INNOVATION** *Library*

From Thistle Burrs to . . . Velcro

by Josh Gregory

Published in the United States of America by Cherry Lake Publishing
Ann Arbor, Michigan
www.cherrylakepublishing.com

Content Adviser: Robert Friedel, PhD, Professor of History, University of Maryland, College Park, Maryland

Design: The Design Lab

Photo Credits: Cover (main) and page 3, ©Stocksnapper/Shutterstock, Inc.; cover (inset), ©Texturis/Shutterstock, Inc.; page 4, ©tale/Shutterstock, Inc.; page 5, ©Antonio Abrignani/Shutterstock, Inc.; page 6, ©photokup/Shutterstock, Inc.; pages 9 and 24, ©auremar/Shutterstock, Inc.; page 10, ©JanBussan/Shutterstock, Inc.; page 12, ©Tomáš Bureš/Dreamstime.com; page 13, ©migstock/Alamy; page 14, ©Science Photo Library/Alamy; page 16, ©The Natural History Museum/Alamy; page 18, ©Stuwdamdorp/Alamy; page 19, ©DWD-photo/Alamy; page 21, NASA; page 23, ©Oramstock/Alamy; page 25, ©Prisma Bildagentur AG/Alamy; page 26, ©Darren Bake/Dreamstime.com; page 27, ©Radius Images/Alamy; page 28, ©Nicholas Burningham/Alamy.

Library of Congress Cataloging-in-Publication Data
Gregory, Josh.
 From thistle burrs to Velcro / by Josh Gregory.
    p. cm. –(Nature's inventors)
 Includes bibliographical references and index.
 ISBN 978-1-61080-494-3 (lib. bdg.) – ISBN 978-1-61080-581-0 (e-book) –
 ISBN 978-1-61080-668-8 (pbk.)
 1. Industrial design–Juvenile literature. 2. Fasteners–Juvenile literature. 3. Seeds–Dispersal–Juvenile literature. I. Title.
 TS171.4.G75 2012
 745.2–dc23   2012001763

Cherry Lake Publishing would like to acknowledge
the work of The Partnership for 21st Century Skills.
Please visit www.21stcenturyskills.org for more information.

Printed in the United States of America
Corporate Graphics Inc.
July 2012
CLFA11

CONTENTS

CHAPTER ONE

Fascinating Fasteners

Velcro is one of the many items that we use every day.

When is the last time you used Velcro? If you're anything like millions of other people around the world, it was probably quite recently. You may have used it to close a flap on your backpack. Maybe you used it to hang a poster on the wall. We use Velcro for so many different things that it can be hard to imagine a time when it didn't exist. However, Velcro was not available until the 1950s. For hundreds of years before then, people fastened things together using other methods, most of which are still in use today.

People have been using buttons to fasten their clothing for hundreds of years.

   One of the earliest types of fasteners was the button. The first buttons were used only for decoration. During the 1200s, people in Europe invented buttonholes and began using buttons to fasten their clothes. At first, only the wealthiest people wore buttons. These buttons were often made of valuable materials, such as ivory, gems, or gold. It was not until the 1700s that simple, cheaper metal buttons became popular. Today, most buttons are made of plastic. While they are useful, they are not the strongest fasteners. They can also take longer to fasten or unfasten, compared to other devices.

Today's buttons come in a wide variety of sizes, shapes, colors, and patterns.

Another early fastener was the buckle. If you are wearing a belt, it is probably held shut using one of these devices. People have used buckles for thousands of years. Ancient Romans and Greeks used them to fasten their armor and helmets. They were once used to fasten almost all shoes and boots. Buckles are very durable and rarely come undone. However, they are also heavy and expensive to make. Though some today are made of plastic, buckles are usually made of metal. They can only adjust to certain sizes, depending on the holes in the connected belts or straps. Buckles are still used for certain things today, but inventors have found better solutions for many of their former uses.

In 1790, an unknown inventor in England came up with a new fastener to replace buckles on footwear: the shoelace. Since then, shoelaces have become the most popular way to secure shoes. Unlike buckles, shoelaces can be adjusted to any size. They can tighten the entire shoe, rather than just the points where a strap crosses over it. Because they are soft and lightweight, shoelaces are also far more comfortable than buckles. Can you imagine trying to run or play sports with metal buckles on your shoes?

If you are wearing jeans or a jacket, or if you carried a backpack to school, chances are you've used a zipper today. Whitcomb Judson, an inventor from Chicago,

Learning & Innovation Skills

Much of what we know about early buttons and other elements of ancient life is thanks to the work of **archaeologists** and historians. Archaeologists dig up **artifacts** at places where ancient people once lived. Because of these scientists' work, many ancient buttons can be seen in museums around the world.

Historians study these artifacts. They also learn a great deal from studying writings and paintings from ancient civilizations. For example, paintings have shown historians exactly which kinds of buttons royalty and wealthy families wore hundreds of years ago.

Illinois, first created this useful fastener in 1893. Judson designed his zipper as a replacement for bootlaces, which took a long time to tighten and tie and came undone easily. He based his design on the much older hook and eye fasteners. This fastener had two parts: a small eye, or loop, and a hook that latched into it. Judson's zipper used a series of these fasteners that hooked together in a long line. The zippers jammed easily, but they worked.

In 1913, a Swedish-American **engineer** named Gideon Sundback improved on Judson's design. Sundback created zippers similar to the ones used today. By the 1930s, zippers were being used widely in many different types of clothing. They are fast and easy to use, and they hold together securely. However, even modern zippers can jam from time to time. They might also pinch the user's skin if he or she is not careful.

CHAPTER TWO

All About Burrs

Long before humans invented any sort of fastener, nature had found its own solution. If you have ever gone on a hike through woods or an area with tall grass, you might have noticed small, spiky objects sticking to your clothes. These are burrs. They grow on certain types of plants. Burrs can be difficult to pull off once they have attached to you. Because they are spiky, they are hard to grip.

Have you ever found burrs on your socks or pants after a hike?

Wind can carry dandelion seeds far from their parent plant.

Some even have poison that makes you itchy if they poke you. Burrs can be a huge pain for people who like to hike in the woods, but these pesky little things serve a very important purpose for the plants that produce them.

Plants **reproduce** using seeds. These seeds must find their way to healthy soil to be able to grow. Because plants cannot move on their own, they must rely on outside forces to move their seeds around. Some, such as dandelions, depend on the wind to pick up their light, fluffy seeds and blow them to new areas. Other seeds are eaten by animals and later passed as waste after the animal has moved to another location. Plants that grow together in close groups often just drop their seeds directly on the ground.

Some plants use burrs to spread their seeds. Burrs are fruits. This means that they contain the plant's seeds. Burrs are covered in tiny spikes that have hooks at their ends. As animals brush past the plants, the hooks get stuck in their fur. The animals go about their business, and the burrs eventually fall off somewhere away from their parent plant.

Learning & Innovation Skills

Some plants can produce hundreds of burrs at a time. That doesn't mean the burrs will all grow to become new plants. Most seeds never find a place to grow. Plants must produce very large numbers of seeds to ensure that even a few of them grow successfully.

Many different kinds of plants have burrs. As a result, burrs come in a variety of sizes and shapes. Most are either round or football-shaped. They are usually either green or brown. For millions of years, they have played an important role in the survival of many plant **species**. In the mid-1900s, they also became the model for one of the greatest inventions in recent history.

Many types of plants use burrs to spread their seeds.

CHAPTER THREE

An Idea Takes Shape

On a pleasant day in 1941, Swiss engineer George de Mestral put on a wool jacket and thick socks and took his dog for a walk. The two made their way through the woods outside the city of Geneva, Switzerland. As de Mestral hiked, he noticed that a large number of burrs had gotten stuck to his clothes. Looking at them, he was struck with an idea.

De Mestral returned home. He used a microscope

A walk through the woods near Geneva, Switzerland, changed George de Mestral's life forever.

Burrs hold strongly once they are stuck to fabric.

to carefully examine the connection the burrs had formed with his clothing. He noticed that the tiny hooks at the end of the burr spikes had gotten caught on the fibers of his clothes. This was very similar to the way hook and eye fasteners work. De Mestral was amazed that such a tiny thing could have such a strong hold. He wondered if it would work with several more hooks spread across a greater **surface area**. De Mestral began to think about creating a man-made version of a burr's simple hook system. He knew that if he were successful, the device would be stronger and easier to use than most other types of fasteners.

Over the next several years, de Mestral experimented with reproducing the unique ability of a burr's hooks. His idea was to create two separate pieces. One would have a hooked surface similar to that of a burr. The other would be covered in loose loops of fiber.

When placed together, the hook piece would attach securely to the looped piece. However, creating the two pieces was not as simple as de Mestral had hoped. It was incredibly difficult to make the two sides match up properly. In most of his early experiments, either the hooks were too big for the loops or the loops were too big for the hooks. He tried using different materials but had little luck.

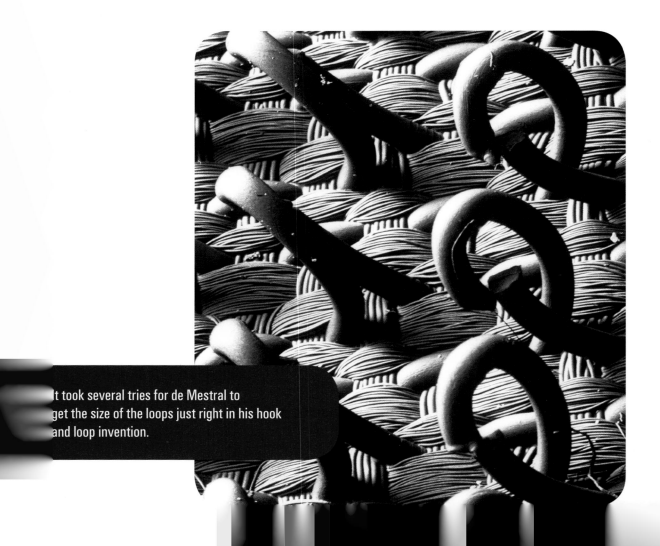

It took several tries for de Mestral to get the size of the loops just right in his hook and loop invention.

De Mestral reached out to a weaver in the town of Lyon, France, for help. Working together, they created a cotton fastener that held together just as de Mestral had planned. However, cotton is very soft. The cotton fastener could only be reused a few times before hooks started breaking and its grip started to weaken. De Mestral wanted to make his invention sturdier.

Now that he had learned the proper sizes for hooks and loops, de Mestral began searching for the perfect material for his new device. Eventually, he discovered that **nylon** could be formed into incredibly strong hooks if it was sewn under the heat of **infrared light**. In 1955, de Mestral put the finishing touches on his invention. The final version had 300 hooks on every square inch of material. It was just as fast and easy to use as de Mestral had hoped it would be.

Later that year, de Mestral received a Swiss **patent** for his fastener. He named the product Velcro, a combination of the French words *velours* and *crochet*, which mean "velvet" and "hook." Soon, de Mestral also received patents in Great Britain, the United States, and many other countries. He quit his day job and took out a $150,000 bank loan to start a company to manufacture and sell Velcro. People around the world began finding many uses for the new fastener. The product was an incredible success.

It did not take long for people to begin coming up with new uses for Velcro.

CHAPTER FOUR

More Useful Than Ever

Today, more than 60 million yards of Velcro are sold each year. Creative inventors have found countless uses for de Mestral's amazing fastener. Others have found ways to improve how Velcro works. Velcro strips with sticky coating on the back can be attached wherever they are needed. The fastener can also be made from materials other than nylon, including

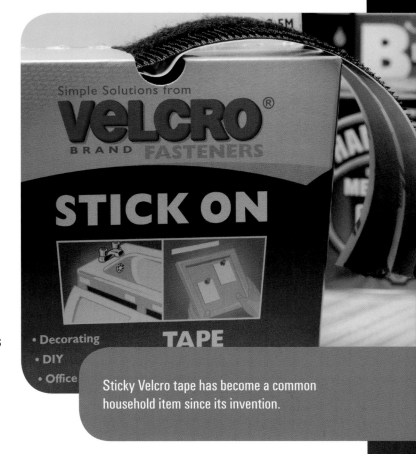

Simple Solutions from
VELCRO ®
BRAND **FASTENERS**

STICK ON

TAPE

• Decorating
• DIY
• Office

Sticky Velcro tape has become a common household item since its invention.

steel, silver, and plastic. Metal Velcro can be used in extreme heat without melting.

One of the product's earliest adopters was the U.S. National Aeronautics and Space Administration (NASA). During the 1960s, NASA was hard at work on the Apollo program, which aimed to land humans on the moon for the first time. Velcro was still a new product. It had not quite caught on with the general public yet. However, the engineers at NASA realized that hook and loop fasteners could be incredibly useful in space, where there is no gravity to hold objects down.

The astronauts of the Apollo program used Velcro often while traveling through space. They used it to attach tools to their clothes to keep the tools from floating away. Velcro on the soles of their shoes helped astronauts keep their feet on the floor. They even used it to attach themselves to the walls of the spacecraft when they wanted to sleep. NASA also used Velcro in the construction of its space suits. The fasteners allowed astronauts to put on or remove their bulky suits with ease. Astronauts also found an interesting use for Velcro's hook side. By putting a piece inside their helmets, they could use it to scratch their faces when they got an itch, even while wearing full space suits!

Velcro became so closely associated with the space program that many people believed that NASA engineers

The astronauts of *Apollo 11* used Velcro on their amazing journey to the moon.

 In 2007, a 66-year-old inventor named Leonard Duffy revealed a new type of fastener. Called the slidingly engaging fastener, the device has two sides with different surfaces, just as Velcro does. Both sides are made of plastic and are covered in shapes that slide together and lock into place. Unlike Velcro, the slidingly engaging fastener does not make any noise when it is pulled apart.

Duffy spent eight years perfecting the design. Since getting it just right, he has been working with several different companies to create products that use his fastener. One day, it could be just as popular as Velcro.

had invented it. Although it inspired these false rumors, the space program made Velcro a much more popular product. NASA's inventive uses for it sparked the imaginations of people everywhere. Soon, other companies began making their own hook and loop fasteners. Because Velcro was patented, these other versions had small differences. But the basic function of all hook and loop fasteners was the same.

Few people at the time used these fasteners for de Mestral's original purpose. He had planned for his invention to replace zippers and other clothing fasteners. This use failed to catch on. Many people did not like that Velcro wears out or the noise it makes when it is pulled apart.

This opinion began to change as time went on. Today, it is used in a variety of clothing and fashion accessories. It holds bags tightly shut and keeps watches on wrists. Some people use it to fasten their shoes. Its light weight and lack of any hard pieces make it perfect for sports clothing.

Many people prefer Velcro shoes because they do not take as long to put on as shoes with laces do.

Today, Velcro is used as both a clothing fastener and a tool. It has even been used in medical operations! Doctors used it to hold the pieces of the world's first artificial heart together when they placed the device inside their patient. This incredible invention has truly been everywhere. Only time will tell what amazing new uses people will find for it in the future.

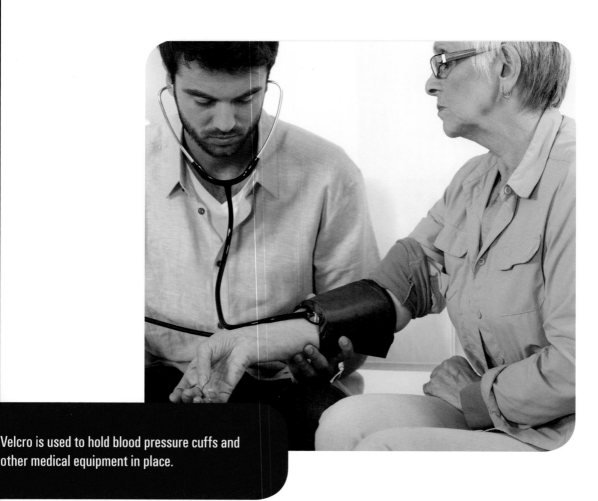

Velcro is used to hold blood pressure cuffs and other medical equipment in place.

CHAPTER FIVE

An Incredible Inventor

George de Mestral (1907–1990) was born to a working-class family near the town of Lausanne, Switzerland. He began his career as an inventor as a young boy. At age 12, he patented his first device, a type of model airplane. This interest in science and engineering continued as de Mestral grew older.

After high school, de Mestral enrolled in college at a technology school

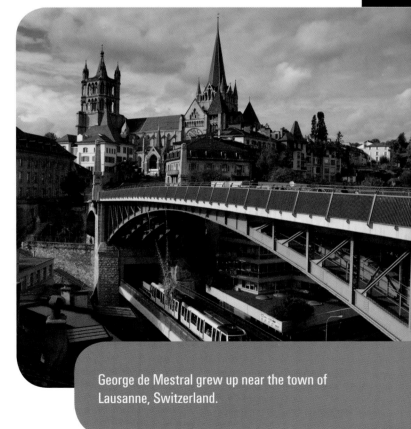

George de Mestral grew up near the town of Lausanne, Switzerland.

Model airplanes were one of the inspirations that led to de Mestral's career as an inventor.

People are constantly finding new uses for de Mestral's invention of Velcro.

near his hometown. He paid his way through school by working a variety of odd jobs, and he received a degree in electrical engineering. His talents soon earned him a job in the machine shop of an engineering company. He went to this job during the day and returned home in the evenings to work on his own projects.

What new and exciting things will you do
with Velcro?

De Mestral was an avid outdoorsman. This led to his invention of Velcro. He quit his job to found Velcro SA, the company that manufactured and sold his fasteners. Because his product was unlike anything ever produced, he had to invent new machines to **mass-produce** it. He expanded the company worldwide, and as Velcro became more successful, it made de Mestral a multimillionaire. Eventually, he sold his company and all of his Velcro patents, choosing to live off his earnings.

Velcro was not de Mestral's only invention. He also designed such gadgets as an asparagus peeler and a device to measure **humidity**. After a long, interesting life, de Mestral died on February 8, 1990, in his hometown. Nine years later, he was inducted into the National Inventors Hall of Fame. Thanks to his invention, he is sure to be remembered for many years to come.

Glossary

archaeologists (ahr-kee-AH-luh-jists) scientists who study past people and cultures by digging up and studying artifacts

artifacts (AHR-tuh-fakts) objects made or changed by humans

engineer (en-juh-NIHR) a person who is trained to design and build machines or structures

humidity (hyoo-MID-i-tee) the amount of moisture in the air

infrared light (IN-fruh-red LITE) a type of light that cannot be seen by the human eye

mass-produce (MASS pruh-DOOS) to make large amounts of identical things using machines

nylon (NYE-lahn) a strong, man-made fiber used to make such things as clothing, carpets, and ropes

patent (PAT-int) the legal ownership of an invention

reproduce (ree-pruh-DOOS) to produce offspring

species (SPEE-sheez) one of the groups into which scientists organize similar animals or plants

surface area (SUR-fis AIR-ee-uh) the amount of space exposed on the outside of an object

For More Information

BOOKS

Becker, Helaine. *What's the Big Idea? Inventions That Changed Life on Earth Forever*. Toronto: Maple Tree Press, 2009.

Bridgman, Roger. *1,000 Inventions and Discoveries*. New York: DK Publishing, 2006.

WEB SITES

National Inventors Hall of Fame—George de Mestral
www.invent.org/hall_of_fame/37.html
Learn more about George de Mestral and his incredible invention.

Velcro
www.velcro.com
Visit the official site of Velcro Industries to learn about the newest uses of George de Mestral's invention.

Index

About the Author

Josh Gregory writes and edits books for kids. He lives in Chicago, Illinois.